The Time
Breakthrough

Library and Archives Canada Cataloguing in Publication

Sullivan, Dan, 1944-
    The time breakthrough : transforming time from a quantity to a
quality / Dan Sullivan.

Includes index.
ISBN 1-897239-04-1

    1. Businesspeople--Time management.   2. Time management.
I. Title.

HD69.T54S94   2006   658.4'093   C2006-905596-3

Printed in Toronto, Canada. January 2015. The Strategic Coach Inc., 33 Fraser Avenue, Suite 201, Toronto, Ontario, M6K 3J9.

This publication is meant to strengthen your common sense, not to substitute for it. It is also not a substitute for the advice of your doctor, lawyer, accountant, or any of your advisors, personal or professional.

If you would like further information about the Strategic Coach® Program or other Strategic Coach® services and products, please telephone 416.531.7399 or 1.800.387.3206. Fax: 416.531.1135. Email: info@strategiccoach.com.

Introduction:
Eliminating the biggest danger facing modern people.

People who reside in modern countries, who work in modern economies, and who live modern lifestyles are confronted with a danger that is literally driving many of them crazy, making others sick, and causing still others to die at an early age. Most of the other problems that modern people face arise from their inability to eliminate this one central danger.

The danger is that they are running out of time in all areas of their lives.

This book, *The Time Breakthrough,* and the audio CD and workbook that accompany it, introduce an entirely new way of understanding and managing personal time. The concept here is radically different from the hundreds of other time management schemes that fill the bookshelves. These other schemes are based on the principle of making the best of a bad situation. They all accept the basic premise that time is scarce.

The Time Breakthrough is based on just the opposite premise: that the time available to each of us is abundant.

Instead of feeling pressured and crazed by modern life, we can enjoy its wonderful advantages. Instead of making the best of a bad situation, we can take a wonderful situation and make it increasingly better.

Part I:
The six "Time Traps" of living and working in the modern world.

"Running out of time" is the subject of countless studies and reports. Almost everyone complains about it. Millions of attempts are made to solve it. It seems, however, that one price that must be paid for being "modern" is the rapid depletion of personal time. This depletion affects not just the quantity of personal time, but the quality.

As the pace of modernization speeds up in the world, the process of time depletion also increases. The forces of modernization increasingly drive people who are living and working in modern society into six different kinds of "Time Traps."

The Six Time Traps

1	Being connected to the 24-hour technological revolution.
2	Exposure to increasing amounts of disconnected information.
3	The temptation or necessity to make increased choices in fixed amounts of time.
4	Having one's work and livelihood commoditized.
5	Dependency on inefficient bureaucratic structures and processes.
6	Having one's lifetime ideals and values trivialized.

Time Trap 1:
Being connected to the 24-hour technological revolution.

We're in the early stages of a technological revolution caused by the microchip. Whenever a new invention is introduced that has wide applications, people use it to increase their capabilities—in this case, their communication capabilities. The popular phrase is "to be connected."

This is seen by most people as a positive thing, and trillions of dollars are currently being invested to increase the connection. Think of the technological devices that have become available to more and more people: the cellular phone, voicemail, and email, to name just a few.

For all of its benefits, being connected also has a negative side. Those involved with the latest technologies find themselves at the mercy of other people's unpredictable demands, agendas, and schedules. The distinction between personal and business time disappears. Instead of becoming more productive because of easier communication, many people find themselves overwhelmed by technological disruptions 24 hours a day. If we're going to live in this world, though, there's no going back: These technologies are too important, too valuable.

People have to develop the necessary strategies to deal with this technological revolution. They have to know how to disconnect, and be able to distinguish between the times when they should be connected and when they shouldn't. They are in Time Trap 1, and they need the knowledge and skills to be able to get out.

Time Trap 2:
Exposure to increasing amounts of disconnected information.

We now live in the so-called Information Age. Some experts claim that the average person doing office work in a large city encounters more new information daily than a well-educated person in the 18th century encountered in an entire lifetime.

It becomes easier and cheaper all the time to use the new technologies to generate, store, and transmit information on every conceivable subject.

The growth of the Internet, with billions of users, means that the amount of information in the world is probably doubling every 18 months. Many people now swim in an ocean of multi-plying information. Each day, they are inundated by tidal waves of disconnected facts and figures. Attention and energy, and *especially time*, are spent sorting through increased amounts of useless information in order to find a bit that is useful. They absolutely must be informed! All the time! Up to the minute!

Can't get enough of it! Might miss something crucial! Life and livelihood depend on it!

This overwhelming volume of information becomes even more of a problem because of the way we have been trained to deal with time: Our whole notion of time impairs our ability to handle these vast amounts of information. We have growing legions of information addicts in Time Trap 2 who can't beat the habit.

Time Trap 3:
The temptation or necessity to make increased choices in fixed amounts of time.

With multiplying amounts of information coming at us from myriad directions, people today are invited or *required* to make more choices. "Choose me! No, choose me! No, I'm newer! I'm better! I'm faster! I'm cheaper!" It comes at everyone, incessantly, every day. Every seller of a product, service, or experience wants the undivided attention of targeted consumers. In the advertising world, this is called achieving "share of mind."

The number of consumer choices people are asked to make —in all areas of life—is bewildering. It wouldn't be a problem if the amount of time they had available kept increasing. Unfortunately, the *quantity of time* available in a day for making choices is more or less fixed. Here's the predicament, then: More and more choices in fixed amounts of time equals *choice overload.*

As this choice overload increases, many people find the *quality* of their time increasingly depleted. A choice today is quickly altered, undermined, or overruled by several more tomorrow. Choices in most areas of life, therefore, are meaningful for shorter periods of time. The Information Age is really the Age of Disposable Choices. Daily life takes on more of a temporary status.

There seems to be no end to this depletion process. It keeps speeding up. As the consumer choices available in the world increase, many people are caught in Time Trap 3 and don't know how to extricate themselves.

Time Trap 4:
Having one's work and livelihood commoditized.

The economist Joseph Schumpeter described capitalism as a never-ending process of "creative destruction." New things are always being created, and old things are always being destroyed. In this dynamic environment, many people are continually fearful for their financial security. As a result, they spend both their working time and private time in a state of anxiety about the future.

The greatest anxiety comes from being "commoditized," which means that one's business or job is measured by a single factor: lowest competitive cost. This occurs when one's product or service can be provided more cheaply with the aid of a technological process. Because of the Internet, which allows for price and cost comparisons of countless products and services around the world, there is always increasing pressure to reduce costs.

Many people find themselves caught in "the commoditization vice": Their customers or employers are searching for ways to replace them—and the only way they can keep their livelihood for the time being is by accepting lower incomes and/or longer working hours. This continual threat undermines their control of time.

As the pace of technological innovation speeds up, so does the process of "creative destruction." More and more businesses and jobs are being commoditized. Increasing numbers of people are caught in Time Trap 4 and can't see a way out.

Time Trap 5:
Dependency on inefficient bureaucratic structures and processes.

In a world of Creative Destruction®, the introduction of new communication technologies continually exposes bureaucratic organizations as inefficient, wasteful, irrelevant, and resistant to progressive change.

Vast amounts of money and human skills are trapped inside these organizations. This is less and less acceptable to the voters, consumers, and investors who pay for the continuation of all bureaucracies. Increased demands for accountability are forced upon all bureaucratic structures and systems in the global marketplace: *Either demonstrate your worth, or disappear.*

This puts enormous pressure on the tens of millions who have bureaucratic jobs. For the past 20 years, there has been a series of shut-downs, takeovers, reorganizations, mergers, and organizational dismemberment—not to mention incessant technological makeover.

Because of downsizing, fewer bureaucrats are expected to do increased amounts of thankless work in an environment of uncertainty, in which they are constantly disrupted by emails, phone calls, and non-productive meetings.

People in this situation suffer burn-out. They have little control over their work and lose their sense of purpose and motivation. They have been bureaucrats for so long—caught in Time Trap 5—they can't imagine being anything else.

Time Trap 6:
Having one's lifetime ideals and values trivialized.

We may be living in the Age of Information, but it would be better if it were the Age of Wisdom. Information is only good for a short time, but wisdom lasts for centuries. We can see this in the words of great teachers that are as meaningful today as when written thousands of years ago.

It is crucial for us to have wisdom in our lives because it allows us to remain focused, confident, and serene during turbulent and confusing times. A lack of wisdom in the midst of information overload—where time seems to speed up—can lead to anxiety, erratic behavior, and physical illness. Without wisdom to guide our thinking, we make bad choices, invest in the wrong activities and relationships, misuse our talents, and waste our opportunities and resources. This Age of Information is also a period during which many highly educated individuals in the public eye are cynical about traditional wisdom. It has become fashionable on television and in the movies to trivialize things that are traditional, sacred, and profound. The cynics, who can be clever and are considered trendy, are especially hostile toward spiritual rules and practices. They make fun of people who profess adherence to centuries-old values and ideals. As a result, it becomes more difficult to teach children about these matters and more difficult for adults to base their lives on them.

Increased information does not necessarily add up to more wisdom. It frequently prevents existing wisdom from being utilized. Many individuals today are searching for a way out of Time Trap 6, but don't know where to begin.

Part II:
The Time Breakthrough: managing time in an entrepreneurial fashion.

Each of the six Time Traps is the result of a fundamental change over the past 25 years in the way that modern life is organized and evolving. This change can be characterized as moving from a "top-down" to a "bottom-up" society.

Top-down.
Throughout the industrial era of the past century, modern societies have been governed by bureaucratic thinking and behavior. This meant central planning and control; in other words, "top-down." A few people at the top controlled the time, activities, and opportunities of those below. Society was thought of as a pyramid with many levels. Most people saw themselves as subordinates in the pyramid, spending their whole lives inside rigid bureaucratic structures and processes. Governments, corporations, unions, religions, non-profit organizations, universities, and school systems all conformed to this model.

Bottom-up.

Because of the widespread use of microchip-based technologies, however, these command-and-control organizations are incapable of responding to changing political, economic, and social conditions. Bureaucratic thinking is now seen as the root cause of many problems and crises. At the same time, there is new entrepreneurial thinking and behavior taking root throughout society, based on the spread of new technologies. Instead of society being seen as a pyramid, it is increasingly being seen as a network. Instead of being top-down, we are moving toward a bottom-up way of arranging our working and living relationships.

A new Entrepreneurial Time System.

Instead of a few superiors giving directions, everyone is now expected to be more self-directed in order to take advantage of the networking power of the new technologies. This means managing one's own time, activities, and opportunities. It means looking at oneself as an entrepreneur rather than as a bureaucrat. In order to change one's attitudes, a new kind of time system is required, *an Entrepreneurial Time System*.

Over the past 40 years, I have personally worked closely with over 6,000 highly successful entrepreneurs in 60 different industries, from a dozen different countries. This work, involving over 25,000 hours of in-depth discussions, has evolved into a unique time management system that enables entrepreneurs to do the following:

(1) *Simplify and achieve balance between every aspect of work and personal life.*
(2) *Focus on the Unique Ability activities that lead to the greatest productivity, achievement, contribution, and satisfaction.*
(3) *Transform their Unique Ability into an equally unique economic process that creates the greatest value in the world.*

On the following pages is a description of this Entrepreneurial Time System and how it bypasses the Time Traps of the modern world.

Part III:
The Entrepreneurial Time System®: Free, Focus, and Buffer Days.

The Entrepreneurial Time System is a synthesis of ancient wisdom and the economic advantages offered by technological progress. On the one hand, it restores the notion of "off-limits" days, so that people living in the modern world can cultivate the spiritual and creative dimensions of life. On the other hand, this new system transforms the concept of how work is done—focusing on "best results" and on preparation.

Although The Entrepreneurial Time System® was created out of many years' experience working exclusively with entrepreneurs, it is now becoming extremely useful for those in bureaucratic situations who are being forced by global changes to adopt entrepreneurial attitudes and methods. In order for non-entrepreneurs to take advantage of this new system, however, it is important to understand how it differs from bureaucratic approaches.

Time management in bureaucratic structures continues to stress the importance of uniformity, conformity, and control.

The Entrepreneurial Time System focuses on the development of leadership, relationship, and creativity among all individuals. Bureaucratic systems are based on a mechanical model, with human beings treated as replaceable machine parts. In The Entrepreneurial Time System, human beings are seen as irreplaceable, never-ending sources of unique value creation. Bureaucratic time systems are designed for static maintenance; The Entrepreneurial Time System is designed for constant innovation and growth.

The three time frames.
The Entrepreneurial Time System consists of three main time frames, which are called Free Days, Focus Days, and Buffer Days. The diagram at the right illustrates these components. Each of these time frames helps to develop a different part of an individual's overall capability. Free Days™ reinforce those activities that expand and rejuvenate the spiritual and creative capabilities. Focus Days™ are designed

to increase productive capabilities, especially those related to increasing income and wealth. The third time frame, Buffer Days™, is for preparation to increase the quality of all activities through planning, practice, and rehearsal.

Each of these time frames is described in greater detail on the following pages.

Free Days™: "off-limits" days for achieving greater rejuvenation.

When people reach the end of their lives, they seldom lament that they didn't spend more time at the office or on the job. Instead, they look at how they dealt with their most important relationships and how they made use of their talents. They reflect on what they contributed to make the world a better place. Most of all, they

judge themselves on the quality of their lives. Did they live life to the fullest? Or was it a life focused only on work?

Making oneself young again.
In The Entrepreneurial Time System, the most important
component is Free Days. These are the off-limits days that
allow people to continually expand their awareness and
enjoyment of life.

By setting aside and taking Free Days, people are able to
rejuvenate themselves—physically, mentally, emotionally, psy-
chologically, creatively, spiritually, and in their relationships.

The word "rejuvenate" comes from the Latin word juvenis,
meaning "young." Individuals who make Free Days the central
focus of their time management stay young no matter what
their age. On the other hand, those who only live a life of work
are old before their time.

A Free Day™ is a whole day, from midnight to midnight, during
which there are no work-related phone calls, meetings, discussions, paperwork, reading, or writing. No number crunch-
ing, brainstorming, or problem solving. Instead, your time and
attention are freed up to explore and enjoy all the activities that
lie outside of work.

Taking great Free Days is an ability that continually improves with practice—an ability that is its own reward. The moment you take a true Free Day, you immediately feel rejuvenated. You are instantly motivated to continually increase the number of your Free Days to gain greater rejuvenation.

Working to live, not living to work.

During these increasing Free Days, you begin to develop a deep appreciation for the non-work side of your life. At the same time, you begin to see the working side of your life in a proper context: More and more, you work to live rather than live to work.

Within the Strategic Coach® Program, many of our entrepreneurial clients confess at the outset that they haven't had a true Free Day in years. But by their third year in the Program, on average, they are able to achieve 150 Free Days.

Focus Days™: "best-results" days for achieving greater productivity.

Let's start by subtracting 150 Free Days from the 365 days in a year, leaving 215 workdays. There are two kinds of workdays: Focus Days and Buffer Days. Buffer Days are used to prepare for Focus Days. This model is based on the entertainment world, which also includes sports. Entertainers and athletes spend a considerable amount of time practicing and rehearsing. By taking time to think through their performance and go through the actual motions, they guarantee themselves a much better performance on the day of the show or the game.

Buffer Days serve the same purpose. They enable sufficient planning and practice for Focus Days. In the Strategic Coach Program, by the end of their third year, entrepreneurs have an average of 80 Buffer Days per year.

"Best-results" days.

By subtracting a further 80 Buffer Days, we are now left with 135 Focus Days. These are focused entirely on achieving the "best results" during workdays. What do "best results" mean? There are now 135 days in which to achieve an entire year's progress and achievements rather than 365. This necessitates much greater efficiency and productivity. In the Strategic Coach Program, this is called strategic urgency—focusing the best abilities on achieving the best results in the shortest possible time.

Apply Unique Ability®.

For entrepreneurs, strategic urgency means first identifying those activities that produce the best results. Invariably, these fall into the area of an individual's Unique Ability®.

Unique Ability activities are characterized by superior skill, passion, extraordinary results, tremendous energy, and continual improvement. A Focus Day™, then, is reserved for the application of these Unique Ability activities—without distractions or interruptions. In other words, 135 days of total focus.

Best opportunities and relationships.

Where should your Unique Ability be focused? On the best opportunities, both short-range and long-range, and on the crucial relationships that offer these opportunities. The success of a particular year always depends on a number of opportunities that are captured and maximized. Let's say there are 40 best opportunities. When you can plan and schedule 135 days for using your Unique Ability, and totally focus these days on these 40 opportunities, you can produce extraordinary results. Your best results, then, are defined by your best possible use of 135 Focus Days in a year.

Buffer Days™: preparation for high-quality Free and Focus Days.

The two most highly-paid and celebrated pro-fessions in the world are sports and entertain-ment. Why is that? Athletes and entertainers do something radically different with their time than other people do: They spend a great deal of focused time preparing for their performances.

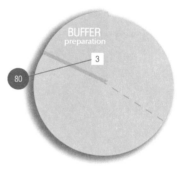

Focus all energies.

Where most people in their daily work just perform, day in and day out, athletes and entertainers devote large amounts of time to practices and rehearsals. This enables them to focus all of their energies on the game, the show, or the concert. The preparation time may be days, weeks, or months, while the actual performance takes just a few hours. In The Entrepreneurial Time System, the "practice and rehearsal" time is taken on 80 Buffer Days, so the best possible "performance" can be achieved on 150 Free Days and 135 Focus Days.

Preparing for Free Days.
In order for a Free Day to be as rejuvenating as possible, Buffer Days are utilized to clean up all details and delegate all responsibilities. Now you can take free time with a clear mind. The goal is to enjoy all Free Days with no need to think about work.

Preparing for Focus Days.
In order for a Focus Day to be as productive as possible, Buffer Days are utilized to complete all background work and preparation. This way, you can perform at that crucial time with clarity and confidence.

Each of the three days—Free, Focus, and Buffer—represent an area of skill. Once you understand what Free Days are, you have the opportunity to get better and better at rejuvenating yourself.

The same is true for Focus Days. Once you understand how they increase productivity, you can keep increasing their power.

Increasing the skill of preparation.
In the case of Buffer Days, there is a constant increase in the skill of preparation. This means that whole days are taken just to prepare your mind and organize your activities. The more you develop this skill, the greater your performance and results.

The people who are skilled at taking Buffer Days give themselves permission to step back and look at the important events—Free and Focus Days—that lie ahead. They realize that their whole year consists of handling a certain number of crucial situations in the best possible way. They see themselves as performers, just like athletes and entertainers. They use their Buffer Days to practice and rehearse, so that when performance day comes, they can put on the best possible show.

PART IV:
Escaping from the six Time Traps.

We are currently in the midst of what I call a Great Crossover®. This started with the widespread introduction of the microchip in the 1970s and will continue until the majority of *top-down* organizations in the world have been replaced by ones that are *bottom-up*. This will probably take the entire 21st century.

The most fundamental progress.
During this period, the entire global population will be weaning itself off bureaucratic structures and adopting entrepreneurial attitudes and methods. Since time is the one thing that all human beings have in common, the most fundamental progress in this Great Crossover will be made first in how each individual manages his or her time. The Entrepreneurial Time System will be a crucial tool for people to make the necessary transformations in their thinking and behavior.

Antidote to bureaucracy.

The bureaucratic world will not disappear quietly or easily.
Enormous amounts of effort and resources will be devoted to
keeping people within its structures of control.

The six Time Traps described in Part I all represent the ways in
which people are still being prevented from using their intelli-
gence, creativity, and abilities in a more entrepreneurial fashion.
But The Entrepreneurial Time System—based on Free, Focus,
and Buffer Days—is an immediate antidote to bureaucratic
thinking. The moment people start planning, organizing, and
acting in this new fashion, they begin to escape from the Time
Traps.

Able to disconnect.

The use of Buffer Days to prepare for your most important performances and to make Focus Days be extraordinarily productive means that you don't have to be connected all the time.
Larger results are achieved more quickly. You have more Free
Days, which enable you to "disconnect" and rejuvenate.

As you use The Entrepreneurial Time System and become more rejuvenated, creative, and productive, you find your work is based more on strategic wisdom and opportunity.
You are able to ignore most of the useless information that overwhelms and paralyzes the bureaucratic world.

As the daily connections and information decrease, so do the number of choices. Life gets simpler and calmer, less reactive and more proactive. Choices become more strategic, integrated, and lasting.

As Free, Focus, and Buffer Days become a way of life, the value of daily work increases. "Busy work" is eliminated, replaced by unique value creation. Individuals become immune to the forces of commoditization.

All of this leads to a life that is just the opposite of bureaucratic existence in the 21st century. Instead of feeling trapped, individuals using The Entrepreneurial Time System find their lives becoming increasingly rejuvenating, creative, integrated, and enjoyable—based on timeless values and principles.

PART V:
The 21-Day Time Breakthrough™

Free Days, Focus Days, and Buffer Days are habits, and habits of any kind are established through the repetition of specific activities over a period of time. Twenty-one days is usually considered the minimum duration. When you repeat something daily over a three-week period, the activity begins to feel natural and normal. It begins to feel like you have been doing it for much longer. You also begin to experience the activity as an automatic part of who you are. It will be easy to continue doing it.

The habit workbook.
There are three tools for The Time Breakthrough: this mini-book, an audio CD, and *The 21-Day Time Breakthrough* workbook.

The 21-Day Time Breakthrough workbook is an opportunity for you to put the concepts of this presentation into practice. Use it to establish Free, Focus, and Buffer Days as habits in your life through a daily exercise repeated over a three-week period. From the very first day you do this exercise, you will

notice an increasing awareness of the usefulness and power of each one of these days. There will be an increasing sense of rejuvenation, preparation, and productivity. After 21 days, you will have made tremendous progress toward a life in which the time to do all the things you love and enjoy is abundant.

PART VI:
The Strategic Coach® Program.

New times require new kinds of education. The microchip revolution is vastly increasing entrepreneurial and consumer activity in global society. This is putting unbearable strains on traditional educational systems, which were designed for simpler societies where individuals had fewer choices.

The traditional emphasis has been on bringing individuals into lifetime conformity with inflexible agrarian and industrial institutions. The new emphasis is on enabling individuals to be flexible, adaptable, innovative, and responsive in a world of changing institutions. The Time Breakthrough is a tool that enables individuals to thrive in this world.

A lifetime program for achieving greater simplicity, balance, and focus.
The Time Breakthrough is just one of many Knowledge Products and programs provided by Strategic Coach®, an organization dedicated to a new kind of education through the teaching of entrepreneurial knowledge, attitudes, skills, and

habits. Thousands of entrepreneurs, their families, and their support teams are presently taking advantage of programs designed to bring greater simplicity, balance, and focus into their lives.

Further information
For further information on Strategic Coach programs and Knowledge Products, call **416.531.7399** or **1.800.387.3206**. Or visit our website at ***www.strategiccoach.com***.